Do Fire Ants Fight Fires?

How Animals Work in the Wild

For my darling David, who always knows how to put out fires — E.K.

To my parents, for teaching me to find humor in any situation
and to follow what makes me happy — J.P.

Text © 2023 Etta Kaner | Illustrations © 2023 Jenna Piechota
First printing in paperback, 2024

Owlkids Books acknowledges the financial support of the Canada Council for the Arts, the Ontario Arts Council, the Government of Canada through the Canada Book Fund (CBF) and the Government of Ontario through the Ontario Creates Book Initiative for our publishing activities.

Owlkids Books gratefully acknowledges that our office in Toronto is located on the traditional territory of many nations, including the Mississaugas of the Credit, the Chippewa, the Wendat, the Anishinaabeg, and the Haudenosaunee Peoples.

Published in Canada by Owlkids Books Inc., 1 Eglinton Avenue East, Toronto, ON M4P 3A1
Published in the US by Owlkids Books Inc., 1700 Fourth Street, Berkeley, CA 94710

Library of Congress Control Number: 2022937965

Library and Archives Canada Cataloguing in Publication
Title: Do fire ants fight fires? : how animals work in the wild / written by Etta Kaner ; illustrated by Jenna Piechota.
Names: Kaner, Etta, author. | Piechota, Jenna, illustrator.
Description: Previously published in 2023.
Identifiers: Canadiana 20230561756 | ISBN 9781771476935 (softcover)
Subjects: LCSH: Animal behavior—Juvenile literature. | LCSH: Animals—Adaptation—Juvenile literature. | LCSH: Animal defenses—Juvenile literature. | LCGFT: Instructional and educational works. | LCGFT: Picture books.
Classification: LCC QL751.5 .K364 2024 | DDC j591.5—dc23

Edited by Stacey Roderick
Designed by Danielle Arbour
The display typeface in this book is Manhattan Hand, courtesy of Noble People

Manufactured in Guangdong Province, Dongguan City, China,
in January 2024, by Toppan Leefung Packaging & Printing (Dongguan) Co., Ltd.
Job #BAYDC112/R1

pb   B   C   D   E   F   G

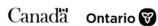

Publisher of Chirp, Chickadee and OWL
www.owlkidsbooks.com

Owlkids Books is a division of bayard canada

Do Fire Ants Fight Fires?

How Animals Work in the Wild

Written by **Etta Kaner**

Illustrated by **Jenna Piechota**

Owlkids Books

Animals have to work hard to survive. Do they go to the office to do their work?

So how do animals work?
Let's find out...

Do fire ants fight fires?

Fire ants *make* fires—in a way. They use a burning venom to sting their prey (the animals they eat). And watch out! They will also sting people and animals that walk on or near the mounds they build.

Do vultures collect garbage?

Vultures are nature's cleanup crew. They eat the flesh of dead animals that becomes stinky if left to rot, and can spread disease. But don't vultures get sick from their rotten meals? Nope. Their stomach acids (liquids that help digest food) are strong enough to kill germs.

Do damselfish grow food?

YES!

Damselfish are picky eaters. That's why they work hard to take care of their favorite food—the red algae that grow in the coral reefs where they live. Damselfish use their teeth to weed out other algae they don't like and dump them away from their "farms." They also protect their red algae crops from intruders. But mysid shrimp are always welcome. Their poop helps the algae grow!

Do moles build subway tunnels?

But maybe they should. Moles can dig their tunnels three times faster than the machines that dig under our cities! Their wide front paws and long sharp claws are perfect for pushing away dirt and pressing it against tunnel walls. For moles, creating maze-like tunnel homes is a snap!

Do monkeys bake bread?

Brown capuchin monkeys don't bake bread, but they do bake palm nuts. The tasty part of the nut is inside a tough shell. To get at it, the monkeys use their teeth to strip off the husk covering the shell. Then they leave the nut in the sun for about a week. Now the "baked" nutshell is dried out and can be cracked open with a heavy rock. Yum!

Do spiders drive school buses?

But female wolf spiders *do* carry their young around on their backs. A mother spider might have to lug around as many as a thousand spiderlings at a time! She does this for up to two weeks after the young spiders hatch. This way, a spider can protect her young from predators (animals that want to eat them) until they are strong enough to look after themselves.

Do tapirs deliver packages?

YES! (SORT OF)

South American tapirs travel long distances, delivering seed-filled poop packages as they go. They wander from one part of the rain forest to another, eating fruit from trees. Along the way, they poop out the fruit seeds that are too hard to digest. This is the perfect way to help new trees grow—seeds and fertilizer all in one package!

Do puffer fish create art?

YES!

Some male puffer fish create fancy designs in the sand on the ocean floor. And all they use to make these huge patterns are their small fins! A puffer fish will work all day and night for a whole week so the ocean currents don't have a chance to destroy his masterpiece. Why does he work so hard? To attract a female who will want to lay her eggs in the center of the design.

Do frogs act in movies?

NO!

But spotted litter frogs do sometimes act…like they're *dead*. Usually, these frogs try to hide or hop away from predators. But if they can't avoid the danger, they flip over on their backs with their legs in the air. Not only that, these frogs also *smell* like they're dead. Eww! No predator wants to eat a frog that might have died from a disease.

Do dolphins teach?

YES!

Atlantic spotted dolphin mothers teach their young calves how to fish. With her calf at her side, a mother dolphin uses her beak to disturb fish hiding in the sandy ocean floor. Then she shows her calf how to chase prey. Often, she lets the fish get away and starts all over again with another one. After all, practice makes perfect!

Do prairie dogs lock up bad guys?

NO!

But prairie dogs are always on the *lookout* for bad guys— predators such as badgers, coyotes, eagles, ferrets, and snakes. As soon as they see one, they bark a loud alarm call to other prairie dogs. This warning describes how big the predator is, how close it is, and how quickly it's moving. The prairie dogs even use a special all-clear call when the threat has passed!

Do birds build apartment buildings?

YES!

Sociable weaverbirds build giant nests that can hold as many as one hundred families. First, a small group weaves a large sloping roof out of twigs near the top of a tall tree. Then pairs of birds use grass stems to add their own round cozy nests to the underside of the roof. Finally, sharp, spiky straws are placed in the entrance tunnel to keep sneaky snakes away.

Do mongooses babysit?

YES!

Banded mongooses live in groups. That means there are plenty of babysitters around. While other members of the group are away searching for food, the babysitters protect the newborns from predators. After a month, each pup gets a special sitter. It teaches the pup how to look for insects to eat and protects it from danger. Back at the den, the sitter plays with the pup and grooms it. Whew! Babysitting is hard work.

All the animals in this book have
important jobs to do.

What jobs do *you* have
at home or at school?